What's In Your Hands

"Stir into Flame The Gift Within"

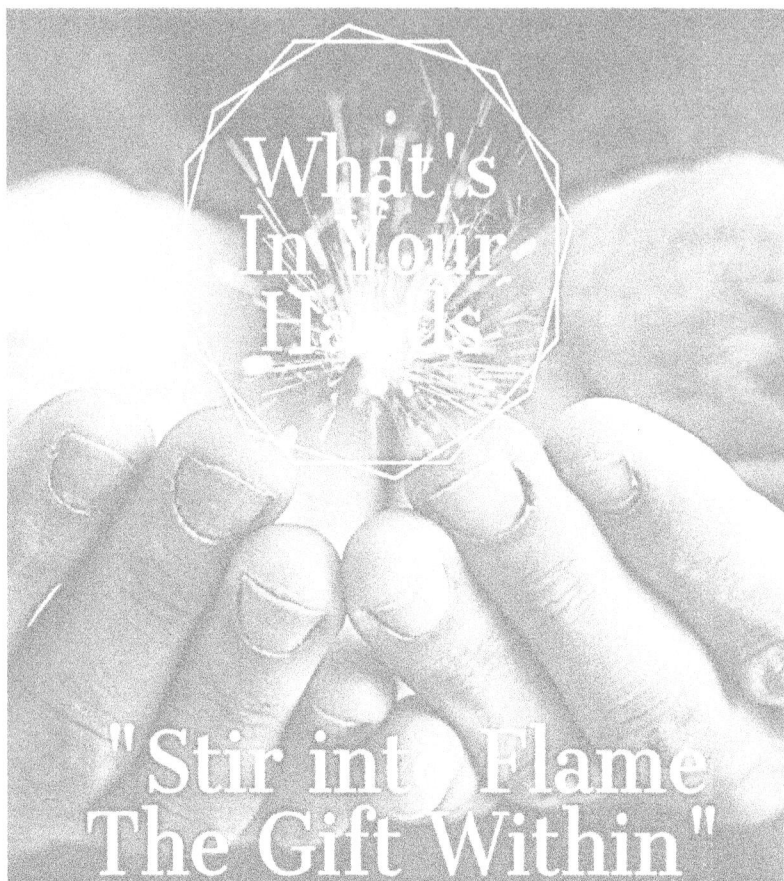

DR. TEMAKI CARR

Published by:

EMPOWER ME BOOKS, INC.

A Subsidiary of Empower Me Enterprises, Inc.

P.O. Box 16153 Durham, North Carolina 27704

Www.EmpowerMeBooks.com

ISBN: 978-1954418004

Printed in The United States of America

This book is dedicated to those who unknowingly carry the flame of God within them...

Your time is Now...

ARISE

FOREWORD

Dr. Temaki Carr is the ready writer as the scribe to enhance the reader for structure in ministry. This book will grab the attention of a listening ear to hear what the Spirit is saying to the Believer. There shall be an activation that will take place to sound the shofar and beckon those to come closer to The Lord and say, "send me."

Isaiah 6:8 (KJV) "Then I heard the voice of the Lord saying, "Whom shall I send? And who will go for us?" And I said, "Here am I. Send me!"

Dr. Fredrick J. Harris
Without Limits Ministries
P.O. BOX 1891
Fuquay-Varina, NC 27526
Phone: (919) 215-2429

ACKNOWLEDGMENTS

I would first like to acknowledge and thank my husband, Robert Carr, whose love, encouragement, and support are like the air I breathe. Secondly, I would like to thank my daughters Dominique, Danielle, and Gabrielle whose unwavering belief that I can accomplish anything propels me forward.

To my mother, Doris Funchess, thank you for modeling and instilling within me a mindset to persevere.

I would like to thank the army of mentors who have walked with me throughout my faith journey. To my earliest mentors, Edrice Polk and Maxine Magee, thank you for introducing me early to a loving and powerful God. To Pastor, Dr. Raymond Bell and the Family of Hope, Thank You for caring for me. To Chief Apostle Frederick Harris and the Without Limits Ministries, thank you for steadfastly "Activating" and calling forth the gift of God within me.

To my publisher and Woman of God, Jessica Highsmith, thank you for your agility and dedication to midwife and bring to life the gifts of many.

Finally, to a powerful group of prayer warriors and friends, Laura Hart, Patrice Hawkins, Charlma Quarles, and Connie Robinson, when you pray, heaven listens and the earth obeys, Thank You.

INTRODUCTION

After Moses led the Israelites from Egyptian enslavement, they were hotly pursued by their former slave masters. For a moment Moses and those he delivered enjoyed a "taste" of total freedom. But after that brief moment of exhilaration the Israelites discovered that their former tasks masters had not truly accepted their freedom and pursued them vigorously. The Egyptians wanted to contain, limit, restrict, and control the Israelites.

Moses stood between angry Egyptians who pursued him and the obstacle of the Red Sea in front of him. He stood between the pursuit of his past, threatening to overtake him and the obstacle of a seemingly immovable sea denying him an opportunity to his future. Moses was afraid. He feared that the past would overtake him, and that the future was simply unattainable.

After all the highs and lows of his improbable journey, how could he now find himself in this type of predicament? Was it all for nothing? Had God abandoned him? How was this moment to end? Moses looked to God...and God asked Him, "What's in Your Hands?"

What pursues you? What is the obstacle before You? "What's in Your Hands?"

WHAT'S IN YOUR HANDS ?

STIR INTO FLAME THE GIFT WITHIN

CONTENTS

CONTENTS

CHAPTER ONE

The Stage is Set to See and Hear the Call

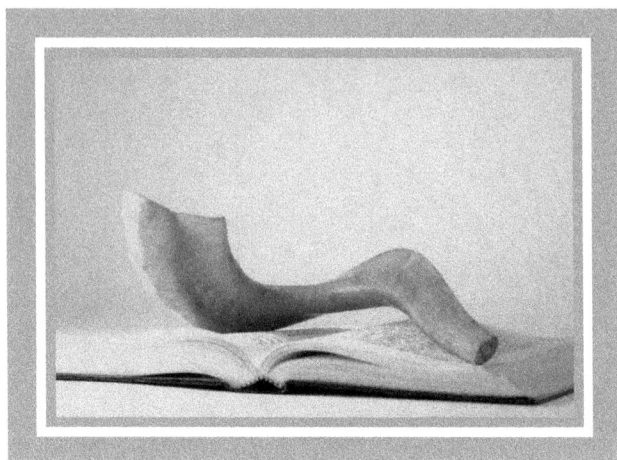

The Conditions are Perfect for a Revealing
Romans 8:19-22

Man of God, Woman of God, Servant of God, the conditions around us are "Perfect" for a revealing. Day after day, we witness more and more hopelessness and despair. Each day conditions around us appear to worsen rather than improve. Division and frustration loom large. Each day our society reaches new levels of intolerance, injustice, and degradation. It seems almost overwhelming. The conditions are just about desperate enough when the people of "The World" and the people of "Faith" are beginning to "Look." They are beginning to "Search" for those who are *Change Agents.*

*Moses, David, Joseph, Elijah, **Jesus**, Martin Luther, Martin Luther King were all Change Agents. You are a Change Agent.*

YOU ARE GOD's CHOSEN CHANGE AGENT.
Allow that to sink in for a moment.

Let us consider "Why" the world is now searching for Change Agents. Let us now consider why people are Looking for YOU. People are looking for Change Agents because the status quo is simply not good enough

2

anymore. People want "Change". The status quo is simply intolerable.

The world Needs a Change Agent who will:

- Point to the "Way of God"
  (and No Other, not even themselves)

- Speak the "TRUTH of God"
  (No Matter What with no agenda)

- Intercede for the "Creation of God"
  (Continuously)

Imposters can talk a good game. They can talk the talk. They can even look the part, but imposters cannot walk the walk. Only True and Authentic God Chosen Change Agents possess that "Special Something" that enables them to walk in the grace and anointing that brings about True Change. That special something enables them, strengthens them, enlightens them to serve as catalysts for change. That special something is called GRACE and ANOINTING. You have it. It is IN You. We need to ACTIVATE it!

It is Time for You to Know Who You Are.
It is Time for You to Take Your Post.

"I Looked for Someone Among them who would build up the wall and stand before me in the gap on behalf of the land so I would NOT have to destroy it…." Ezekiel 22:30

Do You S.E.E. The LORD?
Isaiah 6:1-8

The passage above highlights the Fact that Isaiah "Saw" The Lord. The Prophet Isaiah could SEE the Lord in two entirely different ways. First, he could "SEE" with his eyes as described in the dictionary, "perceive with the eyes; discern visually." Secondly, the Prophet Isaiah could now "SEE" through the eyes of the Spirit. This second type of **SEE**ing allowed the Prophet to:

SEEK ... The Lord
Exalt ... The Lord
Expect ... The Lord

S.E.E.   Seek, Exalt and Expect

Can you SEE the Lord?

Chapters one through five of the book of Isaiah describes the hopeless, dark, and tenuous environment around Isaiah, soon to be Prophet. The Lord saw it all and was very displeased. In fact, God began to call things out with the intention of doing something about it. The intensity to which the Almighty began to call things out would be considered to some as unyielding and severe, even for today's standards.

Highlighted below are just a few of his pronouncements against his own people. The people who were supposed to be intimately familiar with his character and uphold his standard were the exact people who were deceiving themselves while attempting to deceive their God.

This is What God Said in Response:
- ⇒ Your Whole head is injured; your heart afflicted
- ⇒ I have had enough of your burnt offerings
- ⇒ I cannot bear your evil assemblies
- ⇒ You have become a burden
- ⇒ Your hands are full of Blood
- ⇒ Stop doing Wrong
- ⇒ Learn to Do Right

Anything here sound familiar to the environment around us today? Until chapter six, Isaiah could clearly "SEE" the state of everything around him. God showed him the state of affairs of the nation, the heart of the people, the state of the church, and the state of injustice. What Isaiah saw was truly enough to keep him focused on the state of calamity around him.

However, as chapter six begins, we find that there is a "Change in Focus." Note that the situation had "Not" Changed—Isaiah's "Focus" Changed. His perspective, his viewing lens "Shifted" from the disastrous situation, from the who and what of the people, to focus, to See, The Lord.

God is not a 'backstage' or 'behind the scenes' kind of entity.

> When you "SEE" Him...
> HE and HE Alone will become the "PRIORITY."
> HE and HE Alone will become the "FOCUS."

The looming Chaos cannot compare and is out of focus when your heart and spirit Seek, Exalt and Expect (SEE) the majesty of the Almighty taking His rightful place in His Created order. The Prophet Isaiah saw The Lord "High and Exalted." If you cannot "SEE" The Lord, then change your focus and zoom in.

There is a Chain Reaction that happens when we "SEE" The LORD.
1) We S.E.E. The LORD
   (**He is Sovereign and Exalted**)
2) We See Ourselves
   (**We are humbled**)
3) We Hear The LORD

Even now, He asks, "Whom Shall I Send?"
"Who Will Go For Us?"

Calling for The Sent Ones
Acts 10:1-5;9,17,19,20, & 21

"He that has Ears to hear, let him Hear"

In this season, the Sent Ones must <u>leave</u> their places of familiarity, places of comfort, and Break forth to Build the Kingdom of God.

Let us break down our understanding of what places of familiarity and comfort are. First, these are *"NOT"* just geographic/physical places. The dictionary helps us understand this principle:

Familiarity is defined as a "state of knowing something well."
Comfort is defined as a "state of ease and freedom."

Places of familiarity and comfort are also mental, emotional, spiritual, and strategic places of ease, freedom, and knowledge. In the passage above, the Apostle Peter initially operated in a space or an environment amongst those he was well familiar with. He thought he was "Maximizing" the Call on his life. The Apostle Peter thought that he was "Maximizing" the instructions given to him by the

Lord Jesus to Go into all the world and make disciples. However, the truth was that **He had not left the familiar and the comfortable**. *There was More.* *He was Called to do More.* *Are we also like Peter?*

The Lord implores You to: "Expand your Vision" *and* "Stretch Your Tent Wide." Jesus asks you, just as he asked Peter, *"Where are you fishing"?* Are you fishing, casting your net in the same familiar places of comfort spiritually, emotionally, strategically? Are you fishing with the same familiar giftings and knowledge? Are You clinging to the shoreline blending in with the crowd? Are You Trying to Hide?

The Lord bids you to "Launch out to the Deep." The Lord bids you to cast your net on the "other" side. For it is there that so much more awaits. It is in that place in the deep where more intimacy with him awaits, more gifts await, more anointing await, and more fish await.

You probably think that you know who you are, but in the Deep, God will show you who "HE" has really made you to be. From now on, you will be fishers of men—with no limitation and with more anointing. Your Father will show you WHO YOU ARE.

In the passage above, The Apostle Peter was praying and seeking God; he was in a "Position to Hear" and God Spoke. Your Father is speaking now. Do not rationalize it. Do not traditionalize it; HE is CALLING YOU Higher and Deeper. In the passage, The Apostle Peter was needed. Those in need were looking for something He had, something He knew. The situation is no different for you. Someone is in need of YOU, of what YOU have, of What YOU know. Someone is Calling for YOU. THE LORD SENT The APOSTLE. THE LORD is SENDING YOU!

ANSWER THE CALL...

CHAPTER TWO

Let Us Mature and Get Moving

Maturing in Faith: Throwing Off Entanglements
Hebrews 11:33,34 &39   Hebrews 12:1

Maturing in faith and throwing off entanglements are two sides of the same coin. They are a package pair. In order to progress in maturity, there are some things, behaviors, thoughts, characteristics that must be released, cast off or pruned. It may be helpful to review a formal definition of the word maturing.

The dictionary defines maturing in several ways:

1) *To become developed mentally and emotionally and behave in a responsible way.*
2) *Having or showing characteristics, such as patience and prudence, considered typical of well-balanced adulthood*

As we consider the passage above, specifically the first set of scriptures highlighted in chapter 11, we see "maturing faith" demonstrated. This type of faith is developed just as a muscle is developed. It is exercised frequently with an increasing demand of stimulus. Our faith is increased through activation or use. Our faith is not to remain stagnate but to grow in intensity and strength. Just as a muscle. How is your faith being used, developed, or tested at this moment? Do not pull back; step into the development and strengthening of your faith with vigor and confidence.

Maturing spiritually is accompanied by the "releasing" of excess weight, baggage, hindrances, and obstacles to our growth. Releasing implies that there is a choice. You control the release. These things manifest in different forms, sometimes looking as if they are good for us when they are awful for our growth. They can be internal behavioral characteristics or external obstacles, or relationships aimed to slow our progress and maturity. In this passage in chapter 12, we call them entanglements. Let us take a closer look at the formal definition of entanglement and then apply that definition through a spiritual lens. The dictionary defines entangled and entanglement as *Entangled*

1) *Cause to become twisted together with or caught in.*
2) *Involve (someone) in difficulties or complicated circumstances from which it is difficult to escape.*

Entanglement

    1) The state of being entangled.
    2) Something that entangles, confuses,
       ensnares, or delays.

*   While reading this devotional, has the Holy Spirit revealed anything to your heart and mind that is an entanglement? If so, then it is a subtle reminder to "release" that thing. It is an invitation to become "Free" from the entanglement. Maturing in faith requires the release of "all" that stand as obstacles to growth.*

Therefore, since we are surrounded by such a great cloud of witnesses, let us throw off everything that hinders and the sin that so easily entangles. And let us run with perseverance the race marked out for us. ~ Hebrews 12:1

Authentic is The Call
I Corinthians 9:24-26

God has assigned "You" an authentic Kingdom assignment for this hour—this season. He has given you an authentic Kingdom sound. As part of the Kingdom Orchestra, your sound (assignment, gifting) is unique; yet it harmonizes and fits perfectly with the overall kingdom orchestra sound playing at this very moment. Your authentic giftings, skillset, and anointing (grace to do something) are both natural and spiritual. You will need both for this assignment.

RUN <u>YOUR</u> RACE...

Consider Psalms 119:32
I run in the path of your commands, for you have broadened my understanding.

Your Father is expanding your understanding even now. The title of this exhortation is a principle within itself, and every word is essential. Let us examine.

The word "Run" implies <u>Action</u>. Run does not personify a "Sideline" perspective. Examine yourself; see if you are on the sideline or if you are even in the race at all. Did the whistle blow, and you are still at the starting point? Your Father needs YOU in this race.

Run implies a sense of urgency. It implies a full-fledged effort. It implies a full-throttle effort. It is <u>not</u> a lackadaisical (apathetic, careless, or lazy) effort. It implies a <u>focused</u> "PRESS."

Consider Philippians 3:12-14
12 Not that I have already obtained all this, or have already arrived at my goal, but I press on to take hold of that for which Christ Jesus took hold of me. 13 Brothers and sisters, I do not consider myself yet to have taken hold of it. But one thing I do: Forgetting what is behind and straining toward what is ahead, 14 I press on toward the goal to win the prize for which God has called me heavenward in Christ Jesus.

The giftings, skills, and anointing in you are not to be used half-heartedly. Half-heartedness highlights a "Lukewarm" mentality. According to Revelation 3:16, The Lords abhors a Lukewarm mentality or attitude. You are called to win, to dominate. In order to do so, you must Run Your Race.

Let us now examine the specific, authentic Call upon <u>your</u> life. Consider John 15:16
You did not choose me, but I chose you and appointed you so that you might go and bear

fruit—fruit that will last—and so that whatever you ask in my name, the Father will give you.

The Lord has called and chosen YOU. He has appointed, authorized, empowered, gifted, and anointed YOU. He has done all this so that you can "GO" and reproduce. That means that You <u>must</u> "Run Your Race"!

READY... SET... GO!

Reset to Familial Heritage
Luke 2:1-7 ~ (Background Matthew 1:1-17)

You are being called to a "Reset." For a moment, think deeply about that while we take a closer look at a few simple definitions of the word reset.

1) *To set, adjust, or fix in a new or different way.*
2) *To set again, to restore to clear.*

In the passage highlighted above, there were a couple of significant things occurring at once. Joseph was called to return to his (and his father's) family's home of origin, and as this was happening, God used the same event to call the whole of humanity to a "Reset" through the birth of Jesus. In order to restore mankind to himself, to set the "sin record" straight Jesus was born, he ultimately died and rose again to correct the record.

You are being called to a "Reset" via your family heritage. It is not your earthly bloodline but your "Kingdom Bloodline" that has set you up to receive your inheritance. **Your Kingdom Heritage Facilitates the Reset**—*Your true Family is calling for a Reset.*

Where are you traveling from to get to the place of your heritage? Mary was coming from a place of being misunderstood. She came from a place of being ostracized. She came from a place of being mislabeled. She was coming from a place of shame. She had to travel through those places because of "what she carried on the inside of her." **Where are you coming from? What are you carrying inside of you?**

Joseph traveled from a place of embarrassment. He came from a place of folks thinking he was a fool. He traveled through the appearance of desperation. He came from a place of brokenness and separation. He traveled through these places because of what he had to nurture — what he had to protect. **Where are you traveling from? What has your Father given you to protect?**

Joseph traveled "Home" with his new family. Home reminds Us of Who We Are. What Family do YOU belong to that "Activates" the Blessing of God upon Your Life? Home Blesses. The opposite of Blessing is Rejection. If rejection is your portion in this moment, then that place is not "Home." You must get home and reset. When you are home, everywhere you look, there is a reminder of where and how your relatives grew up. Hebrews 12:1 tells us that we are surrounded by a Great Cloud of Witnesses. Everywhere we look, all around us, there are reminders of their Faith and God's Faithfulness to them. Home reminds us of Who We Are.

Perhaps you have forgotten Who You Are. Perhaps, You never really knew. Perhaps you have never really been "Home" before. It is OK! Follow the Sound to Reunite and Reset with Your "True Family" at "HOME." Home Beckons... Come on, Home and Reset.

COME HOME TO DISCOVER WHO YOU REALLY ARE.

CHAPTER THREE

The Value of Brokenness

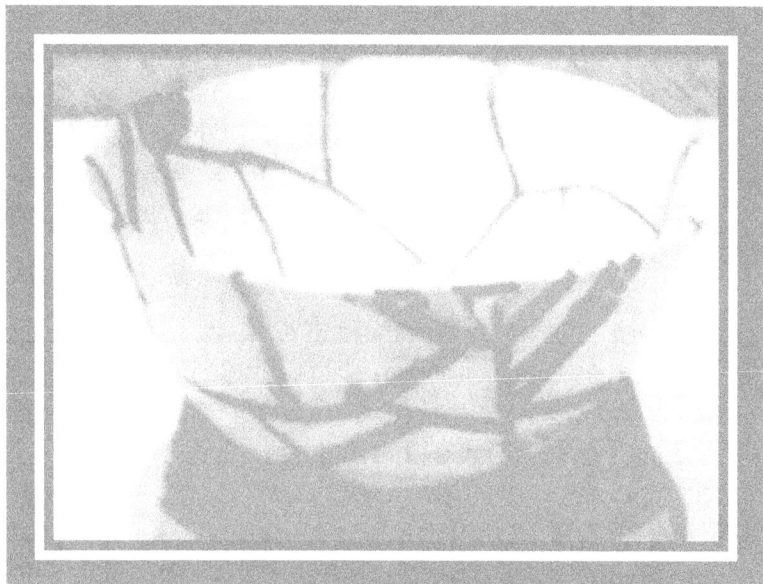

The Beauty of "Brokenness Healed" is a Treasure
for All to Admire.

The Miracle is in Your Brokenness
Isaiah 6:5 ~ Psalms 51:17 ~ Psalms 34:18

In our brokenness, we are able to "SEE." Our brokenness allows us to see God. It allows us to see ourselves. Brokenness allows us to see our Sin—brokenness shepherds in Truth, Humbleness, and Transparency. Brokenness allows us to use these as standards of measure not for others but for ourselves. In our brokenness, we have our Best 20/20 vision. We see things as they are, not as we wish them to be.

Our lens, perspective, or view can sometimes be clouded, dirty, and or obscured by the sin of pride. Brokenness removes the calluses of sin from our perspective. Sometimes we cannot see our sin because it masquerades, hides, or lies dormant, but brokenness forces it to the forefront, allowing us to "SEE" what God sees.

Our Father can see what attempts to hide within us. He can see the Sin of Pride, which we are unable to detect. He can see the Sin of Lust of the Eyes, which masquerades inside us. He can see the Lust of the Flesh, which we rationalize. He can see the Pride of Life of which we feel entitled. In order to use "*What Is In Your Hands*," you must release all that competes with the Truth—all that competes with God.

Let us look closely at what HE Sees:

- <u>Lust of the Eyes</u> – Everything that appeals to the insatiable demands of the eye. We have an insatiable attraction to what we "see," whether it is inherently good or bad.

- <u>Lust of the Flesh</u> - Everything that appeals to the carnal and physical appetite. We cannot get enough. It drives us. It is uncontrollable.

- <u>The Pride of Life</u> – Everything that appeals to haughtiness, arrogance, and pride. This includes personal achievement, popularity, success to produce, and Self-sufficient attitude.

The opposite of the list above is love, joy, peace, patience, kindness, goodness, faithfulness, gentleness/meekness, and self-control. These nine attributes are known as the fruit of the Spirit. Within the fragility and transparency of brokenness, God is near, and He intervenes. Within the fragility and transparency of brokenness, God intervenes, and the Miracle begins.

God's reaction to our brokenness is not "Aha" you are broken but rather "Come near my child "through" your humbleness and transparency...your brokenness. Pride makes us think more highly of ourselves than we should. It is a false sense of self.

Transformative Power is received through the Miracle of Brokenness.

"Father, we Thank You for allowing us through your grace to journey <u>through</u> Brokenness. We Thank You for the Gift of Brokenness."

The Value of Our Brokenness is Immeasurable. Brokenness is the fertilizer that helps to yield a massive, bountiful harvest pleasing to our Father.

It was good for me to have been afflicted so that I could learn your decrees. ~Psalms 119:71

The Cry of a Broken Heart
I Kings 19:9-16 ~ Psalms 51:17

There is a pattern we see emerging as we read the Prophet Elijah's cave journey. It is that of Brokenness, Rest, and Restoration. He is broken because the work is hard, the rejection is real, the resentment is filled with anger and hate. Elijah is exhausted and has essentially come to the end of himself. What more can HE do? Have you ever felt like that? There is not only a lesson for the Prophet Elijah on this cave journey, but there is also a lesson for us.

We see that amidst the brokenness, the Prophet had to "Rest" even as he was on the run because the opposition pursued his life. He had to <u>rest</u> even to get to the presence of God at the mountain in the cave. This rest was all-inclusive. It was physical, mental, and spiritual. What pursues you? Rest allows it <u>not</u> to consume you. Sometimes, you just need to "Rest."

We all need rest. Jesus needed rest, and he rested at what seemed to be the most inconvenient of times. After a long day of teaching and healing the sick, Jesus rested on a boat while it traveled to the other side of the lake where others were in need. Unfortunately, a terrible storm arose while Jesus rested.

How could he rest in the storm when the others were afraid for their lives? Do You wonder how you can rest while a storm is raging?

This "all-inclusive rest" allows us the opportunity to enter into the presence of God. In his presence, our mind is not fretful. Our heart is not anxious. In his presence, we can be transparent, and we can "Rest," for he has it all under control. Like the Prophet Elijah, in our transparency, we can tell him how we feel, what we see…we can show him our broken heart. In God's presence, like the Prophet, we can see ourselves and feel God's embrace over the brokenness, storms, and pursuits of life.

In God's presence, we are restored. Our perspective is restored. Our heart is restored. Our energy is restored. Our spirit is restored. Despite the opposition, God restores us to "Complete the Work" despite the complexity of the assignment, despite the storm. Allow your Father to guide you through the journey of Brokenness, Rest, and Restoration.

Brokenness, Rest, and Restoration
The Prophet Elijah indeed could do no more. He was broken; he needed rest and restoration.

He had performed a true miraculous sacrifice on the mountain top opposing false prophets. However, his true sacrifice was a broken and contrite spirit unto the Lord. King David knew something of this type of sacrifice, as highlighted in *Psalms 51:17 My sacrifice, O God, is a broken spirit; a broken and contrite heart you, God, will not despise.*

As we begin to stir up the flame of the gift within our hands, we will journey through brokenness. Like the Prophet Elijah, we will come to the end of ourselves—our own effort or self-preservation and enter the journey of brokenness.

Have You Come to the End of Yourself Yet?

_____

_____

_____

_____

_____

_____

_____

_____

_____

_____

_____

_____

_____

_____

_____

_____

Your It is Finished Moment
John 17:1& 4 ~ John 19:28-30

As Believers, our ultimate objective is to glorify our Father. We accomplish this objective by daily living on purpose and completing the work he has given us. In the passage above, we see Jesus completing his assignment. This moment is his moment of Glory—because he has walked in obedience, even through agony, even unto death. This moment is also the Father's moment because his Son has persevered despite the persecution and obstacles. There are two critical principles Jesus highlights as he completes his life's work.

1) *The singular focus to honor God through obedience above all else.*
2) *To Complete the Work*

It seems strange to declare this particular moment in our humanity a moment of glorification as it is a moment of intense suffering and sacrifice. Our natural ideas of Glory and honor look and feel nothing like this. Nevertheless, it is 'This' moment above all others in which Jesus honored God the most. Once Jesus completed the work, he declared, "It is Finished."

Are you walking through an "It is Finished" moment? It is that moment when you have done what God gave you to do, and you are waiting.

It is the 'in-between' moment of obedience and manifestation of God's promise. It is the 'in-between' moment just prior to your Father manifesting himself on your behalf. **It is the Moment of Expectation.**

The "It Is Finished" moment is a 'Raw Moment'...It is the Moment of TRUTH. It is that moment when your "Faith" in God and what he has said is tested the most. At that moment, you will either stand in obedient expectation or wander off in your mind or heart. You will either look in expectation or begin to question whether He does what he said. You may even question yourself, saying, "why did I do this."

The "It is Finished Moment" can feel like a lifetime instead of a moment. Remember, that looks can be very deceiving at this moment. It is in this moment when it looks as if the enemy has won. In the passage above, it looked like the enemy had the advantage. It looked like it was over. The enemy was gloating and taking a bow.

Like Jesus, your work may be finished, and the enemy may think that he has won. That the situation is hopeless. That it is finished, But GOD IS NOT FINISHED.

Your "It is Finished" Moment is God's Time to Shine. You may be finished, but HE is just beginning. Now is the Time of your Miracle! As a matter of fact, God cannot truly begin until you are finished. For it is only when you "Release It" from your hands and your power that God takes it into his hands.

Did You Walk in Obedience?

RELEASE IT, for IT IS FINISHED !!!

"I have brought you glory on earth by finishing the work you gave me to do." ~ John 17:4

_____

_____

_____

_____

_____

_____

_____

_____

_____

_____

_____

_____

_____

_____

_____

_____

_____

CHAPTER FOUR

Facing You

It is Not About You
Mark 8:31-38 ~ Mark 10:38-39

In the passage above, Jesus exclaims, "Get out of the Way, Satan! You are seeing things merely from a human point of view, not from God's." He made this remark after Peter suggested that maybe Jesus did not have to suffer at all. Peter sounds like most of us. We try to carry out the assignment for our lives seeing and living from a human perspective. In order to bring the Kingdom of God here on earth, this type of seeing and living simply will not work. Has there ever been a time when you have chosen your desire or will over God's? Has this pattern of behavior become the norm?

This type of behavior is not exclusive to Peter; later in the book of Mark, we find James and John "thinking of themselves" also. Just as Jesus reminded Peter, James, and John, we must remind ourselves that it really is not about "us" personally. It is, in fact, all about "HIM" and HIS Kingdom. It is about 'His Will,' 'His Way.' We must move out of the way and ensure that our personal whims are not impeding the progression of the Kingdom. We must get in line, get in order and get in the "Right Posture." It is the posture of humble submission.

The correct posture is the posture of denying yourself. It is the posture of picking up your cross and drinking that cup. The cup is filled with challenges, trials and suffering. The cup is also filled with triumph. Jesus asked James and John, *"Can you drink the cup I drink or be baptized with the baptism I am baptized with?"* If we are honest, we are more like James and John than we would like to admit. We fully embrace the 'Triumph' part of the Cup, but the Sufferings and Trials we could do without. We must drink the "entire cup" as bitter as it may taste.

In drinking the cup—the entire cup, we deny ourselves. Have you ever begun an assignment for The Lord, and it became intense? Have you ever thought that some trials are more than what you signed up for? We must remind ourselves that it is not about us in these moments, and we must drink the entire cup.

In drinking the cup, we deny ourselves. In denying ourselves, we actually "Find" ourselves. We can "SEE" the Kingdom of God with power in this day and age in denying ourselves. Today let us honestly ask ourselves:

- *Do I love myself and my agenda more than I love The Lord?*

- As I seek to become more intimate with The Lord, is there any room for the "Me and My" behaviors?
- Am I competing with The Lord's will, way or agenda?

Remember: IT is NOT ABOUT YOU!

"Get out of the Way, Satan! You are seeing things merely from a human point of view, not from God's." Mark 8:33

_____

_____

_____

_____

_____

_____

_____

_____

_____

_____

_____

_____

_____

_____

_____

_____

_____

Honor and Cultivate the Seed Within in You
Matthew 13:1-9

Although given by grace, the seed of salvation, the seed of faith, and the seed of your giftings, skills, and anointings, came through costly sacrifice. As this important fact is highlighted, we must not only recognize and honor the Sacrifice of Our Lord for the gift of salvation, but we must also recognize and honor the stewards that have shepherded and protected the seed through the generations.

Countless unsung stewards through the generations have faithfully obeyed the Lord's command to "Make Disciples." Many of them did not have titles or formal shepherding responsibilities. Whether the stewards were formal or informal, we are the result on some unsung seed carrier. One, two, or three of those faithful stewards planted, watered, and cultivated seed in each one of us. If you think hard enough, the memory of these ordinary, unsuspecting heroes may come to mind. Let us think about them for a moment.

We can see now that their simple acts of obedience were monumental foundational pillars for building our faith. The faith that we now stand on is the result of the unsung sacrifice of faithful stewards. The details are important, so allow your memory to take you back to remember their visits, calls, time, wisdom, patience, and guidance. Just as Jesus made the ultimate sacrifice for our salvation, he also designated stewards that would encourage, shepherd, and befriend us to help us throughout the life of our faith journey. Their sacrifice is essential. Their sacrifice to plant, water, and cultivate the seed of salvation in us is worth honoring. We must honor the Lord Jesus and the countless unsung Stewards, by Reproducing.

We Honor the Sacrifice by Reproducing

Seed begets fruit, and fruit begets seed. Let us not allow ourselves to break the cycle. We honor by reproducing. Ask yourself, "Where is the offspring to the Seed that was planted in my life"? Has there been a harvest? Did the seed die with me? Did I fail to cultivate that which was planted in me? Did I water the seed and give it sunlight? Did I allow the seed to live?

Are We Trees with No Fruit?

There is a peculiar story highlighted about Jesus and a Fig Tree. One day, he exerted a lot of energy in the temple, turning over money tables, healing the sick, welcoming and validating the sincere worship of children. Afterward, he left the temple and walked out of the city to a suburban area called Bethany. The next morning, he got up early to walk back into the city to the temple to finish the work. As you can imagine, he was hungry and thought that he could satisfy his hunger with fruit from the Fig tree he saw. This was going to be breakfast. It would be his power meal for a day that was leading to his final days. When he got to the tree, he saw no fruit. He immediately cursed the tree. Did Jesus suffer from a hanger attack? The answer is no; he understood that the Tree was not serving its purpose. It had no fruit.

Check the DNA of Your Seed. Does it have Reproductive Legacy?

Early in the morning, as Jesus was on his way back to the city, he was hungry. Seeing a fig tree by the road, he went up to it but found nothing on it except leaves. Then he said to it, "May you never bear fruit again!" Immediately the tree withered.
Matthew 21:18-19

Get Out of Your Own Way, Face the Enemy Within!
Psalms 121:1-8

The Lord is relentlessly and unapologetically committed to "watching" over your life. His watch is impartial. He watches and defends against all enemies, both foreign and domestic, within and without. The enemy is anything or anyone who counters God's purpose, will, way, or kingdom. Let us read with a fresh perspective Psalms 121:3-4.

He will not let your foot slip— he who watches over you will not slumber;
indeed, he who watches over Israel will neither slumber nor sleep.

The hard truth is that sometimes our own thoughts, behaviors, and life choices sabotage our growth process more than outside sources. This is understandably difficult to hear and even more difficult to admit. However, as we grow and mature in our walk and as we seek to use the full scale of our talents, skills, and giftings, we must be willing to admit hard truths to ourselves.

The Bible is filled with so many examples of those who had to admit hard truths about themselves. Let us take a closer look at just a few.

Moses immediately comes to mind. His impatience on more than one occasion made his faith journey difficult. The killing of the Egyptian and the striking of the rock to release water was the mirror that helped him realize that perhaps he had sabotaged himself. David's sense of entitlement had a negative impact to his faith journey. A New Testament example would be the disabled man sitting by the pool of Bethesda. When an opportunity for a miracle presented itself, he found himself making an excuse. Do their behavior patterns sound familiar to yours in some way?

Our Father is relentless to protecting us from ourselves. He offers an opportunity for us to see and admit the Truth. He then ultimately graces us with the strength and wisdom to change, grow, and mature. God saw Moses, David, and the man by the pool in their finished and unfinished states; yet, he gave them an opportunity to grow to His standard. God saw the 'Potential' in them. The Lord can also see the 'Potential' in us as well. However, just like the others before us, we must grow and mature into His Standard.

Yes, The Lord will keep us from "All" harm. Especially the harm we inflict upon ourselves. Let us look again with a fresh perspective of Psalms 121:7

The LORD will keep you from all harm—He will watch over your life.

You are a Servant of the Most High God. He Accepts You, Calls You, Validates You, Endorses You, and Loves You.

GET OUT OF YOUR OWN WAY!

CHAPTER FIVE

Posturing Your Heart

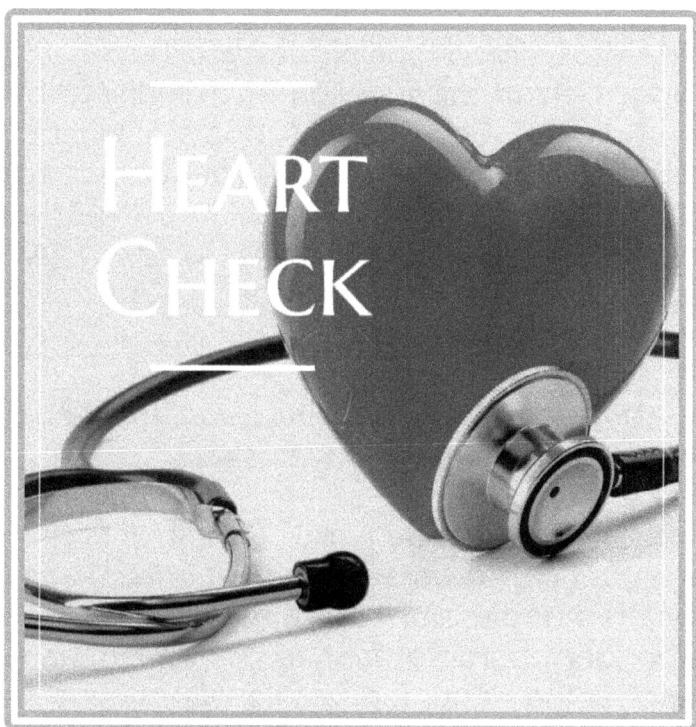

The Power Principle of Love in Action
I John 4:7-8 ~ I Corinthians 13~ John 3:16

Naturally and Spiritually, your heart is one of the most vitally important organs you have. It is the power behind the function of everything, both in your natural and spiritual body. Without the correct function of the heart, your body begins to die. Without the correct function of the heart of your spirit, your spirit begins to die. An old testament proverb provides sage wisdom concerning our heart.

Above all else, guard your heart, for everything you do flows from it. ~ Proverbs 4:23

The Apostle Paul in I Corinthians helps us understand that while our giftings and skills may be anointed and useful, Love is the simplest and most important character trait of all. Our motives are important, and our motives flow from our heart, as highlighted in Proverbs.

We need to realize another fundamental principle regarding Love.

Love, by its very nature, is Action.

Words alone do not demonstrate Love. Thoughts alone do not demonstrate Love. Love is an "Action" Word. Love Requires "Demonstrated" Sacrifice. God the Father exemplified this principle when he gave Jesus as a sacrifice for our sins. The Father loved us, despite our level of ignorant rebellion. He did not just "think" on the Love or "talk" about the love he had for us …HE Actually "demonstrated" his love to us. The crazy thing about God's love is that none of us were in a condition to understand or appreciate his tremendous level of sacrificial love. Think deeply about that for a minute. For it is this same type of Love that He expects us to demonstrate to one another.

While we think about God's standard of Love, let us also list a few other Actionable characteristics about love.

~ Love Compels, Draws
~ Love Permeates Blindness
~ Love is the Guarantor…When all else fails, "LOVE" never fails.

So many things are broken in our world. Sometimes the only solution and the best solution is "Love" according to God's Standard. God's standard of Love is something we do not naturally carry within our human capacity. This type of Love must flow from the Lord's Spirit directly to ours.

As we try to live in God's standard of love, we must remember that :

God's standard of Love Demonstrated is not concerned with whether the receiver "understands" the level of sacrifice. This type of love has the grace to hold its position until...when and if the Receiver comes into the knowledge and understanding of the Gift of Love it has already received.

There is another principle operating when this type of Love is demonstrated. God's standard of *"Love Demonstrated"* is not contractual. Nor is it based upon condition i.e.

If you *"Receive"* my love...
If you *"Understand"* my love...
If you *"Return"* my love...

True Love, Real Love is willing to Allow Time to unpack the layers of its Gift to the Recipient.

... It is not ice, it will not Melt, Dissipate or Disappear in the Hands of the Giver.
... It is not Confined by Events or Conditions. True Love Defies Conventional Limitation

Let Us show this type of Love to Ourselves.
Let Us show this type of Love to All Around Us.
Let Us Be Our Father's Children.

Heart Check: What is in There?
Ezekiel 2:8, 3:3-4 ~ Matthew 18:21-35 ~ I John 4:7-8
~ I Corinthians 13 ~ John 3:16

Are you Heart Healthy? Let us take a moment to examine our hearts. To do so, let us focus upon the principle of a "Stress Test" to see what it reveals. What is revealed from your heart when you are in the test of tribulation. What is revealed when you are trapped in a trial or a snare? Besides God, only you can answer this question honestly.

"Blessed are you when people insult you, persecute you and falsely say all kinds of evil against you because of me. Rejoice and be glad, because great is your reward in heaven, for in the same way they persecuted the prophets who were before you." Matthew 5:11-12

As the scripture above highlights, our focus is not to avoid the snare or the difficulty trial or tribulation; instead, our focus is to persevere through such times with a clean and pure heart. As believers, we all must journey through difficult times. The litmus test is what is revealed in your heart during times of difficulty. What is coming out in the pit, in the snare, in the danger? Whether it is Gushing out, Flaming out, or Oozing out, Check Your heart and understand what is in there.

Do You exhibit mercy, compassion, grace, and patience? Let us take a close look at the definition of mercy. *The dictionary defines mercy as compassion or forgiveness shown toward someone whom it is within one's power to punish or harm.* In the passage in Matthew above, Peter asks, "How many times must I forgive my brother"? Jesus guides Peter to exercise the fruit of mercy and patience. If the Stress Test reveals that our focus, energy, heart, and mouth is not upon God, we have failed the litmus test. If your heart has failed the litmus test in some way, then corrective measures are to be taken.

In the natural, when there is a heart issue, depending upon the severity of the problem, surgery may be necessary. In other remedies may include medication, restrictive diet, and exercise. The same prescriptive measure is to be taken when there is an issue with our spiritual hearts. We must allow the Father to perform surgery on our heart. The medicine is the word of God. We must exercise the fruit of the spirit. We have to change our diets from anger, impatience, and pride to that of humility, mercy and forgiveness.

The Servant of the Lord's Heart must be Humble, Full of Compassion and Ready to Forgive.

Do not let your arteries become clogged, corroded, or FAT.

F ~ Form of Godliness that misses the mark.

A ~ Anger that allows the spirit of murder to crouch at the door.

T ~ Trust issues that have nothing to do with your sinning brother but everything to do with Trusting God.

In the passage above, God told the Prophet Ezekiel to eat the entire scroll, bitterness and all. Like the Prophet,

WE MUST EAT THE ENTIRE SCROLL.
I John 4:7-8 ~ I Corinthians 13~ John 3:16

Posture Yourself on the Side of the Kingdom
Joshua 5:13-15

In the scripture above, we find an interesting situation developing. The Lord had commanded Joshua to cross over into Jericho and seize the land. Before the offensive, he went to scout the territory. He found an unexpected visitor looking and scouting the city as well. Joshua had a simple question: he asked the unexpected scouter, "Are You with Us or Are You with them?   Joshua's question reflects both our attitude and our behavior in life.

Are You with Us or Them?

As the Lord's Servant, the Captain of the Army of Lord demonstrated, This is an irrelevant question, especially when it concerns "Kingdom Work." Angel of the Lord's Army is not sidetracked by anyone's side; his response highlights that our priority must always be "Kingdom Work."   The angel replied, "Neither," his allegiance was to the one who sent him.

Our Allegiance Must Be to the One Who Sends Us

Joshua's response to the Captain of the Lord's Army statement demonstrates our following principle. "Joshua fell facedown to the ground in reverence." WE Must Get Our Posture Right. This means our heart must be correctly postured. Our motives and our actions must align correctly to reverence The Almighty.

What is the position of Your Heart, from which your motives flow? What is the position of your Soul from which your thoughts flow? What is the position of your strength from which your actions flow?

What is the Right Posture for Your Heart?

The right posture of our heart is submission, humility, surrender, worship and openness.

Did you know that it is Possible to Be in the "Right Posture" but ON THE WRONG SIDE? This fact begets the Question: Who or What Are You Posturing For? Is it the side of the Kingdom? Did you know that it is Possible to Be on the Right side but in the "Wrong Posture"?

How do we Get It Right?
Galatians 5:16-26 gives us a clue. Deuteronomy 6:5 sums it up.
Live by The Spirit and ...

Love the LORD your God with all your heart and with all your soul and with all your strength.
ARE YOU IN THE RIGHT POSTURE?

_____

_____

_____

_____

_____

_____

_____

_____

_____

_____

_____

_____

_____

_____

_____

_____

_____

_____

_____

_____

_____

_____

_____

_____

_____

_____

_____

_____

_____

_____

_____

_____

_____

CHAPTER SIX

Take the Hit

When the Leaders and The Crowd Get It Wrong
Luke 23:2 ~ Ezekiel 13

"And They began to Accuse Him, saying "We have found this man Subverting OUR Nation."

The accusers were inciting, exploiting and, manipulating public opinion. These accusers were motivated by the main accuser of the children of God, Satan. The accusers proclaimed that Jesus was "subverting" their nation. Let us take a closer look at the word subverting.

Subverting is defined as undermining the power and authority of an established system or institution.

The accusers said Jesus Claimed to be King. They wanted to know "how" he could Claim this Kingdom authority. As it was with Jesus, so it is with us. We have accusers who get our motives wrong. *"Who mock and challenge our Kingdom authority.?"*
Ecclesiastes 1:9-10 NIV or NTV
"What has been will be again; what has been done will be done again. There is nothing new under the sun" [There is nothing new under the SON either.]

<u>Remember that accusers:</u>
- Incite ~ Encourage or stir up (violent or unlawful behavior)
- Exploit ~ Make full use of deriving benefit from
- Manipulate ~ Control or influence cleverly, unfairly, or unscrupulously.

The entire chapter of Ezekiel 13, God proclaims his judgment to the incitement and exploitation of lying false leaders. The first couple of verses is highlighted below:

The word of the Lord came to me: 2 "Son of man, prophesy against the prophets of Israel who are now prophesying. Say to those who prophesy out of their own imagination: 'Hear the word of the Lord! 3 This is what the Sovereign Lord says: Woe to the foolish[a] prophets who follow their own spirit and have seen nothing!

False accusations were hurled at Jesus. False accusations have come to every Prophet that preceded Jesus. A false accusation will be hurled at us as well. The good news is that Jesus and all the Prophets overcame false accusations, and so will we.

Can You Take the Hit?
Romans 8:28 ~ Genesis 50:20 ~ I Corinthians 9:26

There are times on this journey when the "Servant of the Lord" "MUST" take the HIT. Examples of this principle are :

1) The Hebrew boys in the FIRE
2) Moses at the Red Sea
3) Daniel in the Lion's Den
4) Paul and Silas in Prison
5) Jesus on the Cross

THE HIT is a GUT check.

This means that in your INNERMOST being, "In Your Spirit," you are challenged and asked, "Are You Ready For This Fight? ABSORB THE BLOW.

Listed below are nuggets of intel that highlight the intentions of the Hit:

- to Persuade You that You do not want and could never win this Fight,
- to Discourage You – to convince you that the Fight is too BIG for You.
- Through the story of Joseph, the Scriptures proclaim that "They intended to harm You, to take you out, but instead the HIT actually made you stronger.

The HIT is a Catalyst.   The Hit is Permission to Transform

The HIT was a GUT Check to Show You what the opposition is working with, BUT it is about to show your opposition what YOU ARE working with.

The HIT is the Catalyst to Transformation (H.I.T.)

H ~ Holy
I ~ Internal
T ~ Transformation

Can you Take a Hit, And Return, A Knock-out Blow?

When you take the HIT, Your natural Person may be stunned, But your spirit person is "Ready For The Fight."

When you get HIT: It is an Opportunity to Show "What You Are Working With."

The Giant "Thought" He was Facing a MERE Child in David...But David Had a GUT check and said, "You come at me with a sword...You come at me in the Flesh, But I come at you in IN THE Name of the LORD, OUR GOD.

In other words, David implied, "I am about to show you WHAT I am working with"...On THE INSIDE and "WHO I am working with," Which is The Almighty God.

David demonstrated who the Giant,

"REALLY OPPOSED and that was God.

There are times on this journey when the Servant of the Lord MUST "Take the Hit."

~ What are YOU fighting for?

~ Who are YOU fighting for? —For the crowd, Yourself or God?

~ Who is in Your corner?

~ Are you trainable?

~ Where is your head? Is your head in the fight?

I Corinthians 9:26

"Therefore, I do not run like someone running aimlessly; I do not fight like a Boxer beating the air" (I am not Shadow Boxing)

Romans 8:28 NIV

"And we know that in all things God works for the good of those who Love Him, WHO Being called according to His purpose." OR "All things work together for good to them that Love God to them called according to His Purpose."

Genesis 50:20 NIV

"You intended to harm me, but God intended it for good to accomplish what is now being done, the saving of many lives." OR "You intended to harm me, BUT God intended it all for good. He brought me to this position so I could save the lives of many people."

CAN YOU TAKE THE HIT?

_____

_____

_____

_____

_____

_____

_____

_____

_____

_____

_____

_____

_____

_____

_____

_____

When the Anointing in You Draws Backlash, Remember Who Sent You.

Matthew 10:14 ~ Matthew 10:16 ~ Ezekiel 2:35 ~ Jeremiah 26:2 ~ John 20:21

You are called to Speak, Demonstrate, and Uphold TRUTH.

T ~ Total
R ~ Righteousness
U ~ Unrelenting
T ~ TRUST in a
H ~ Holy God.

If Anyone Does Not Welcome You or Listen to Your Words, Shake the Dust off Your Feet.

Never Allow the TRUTH to Become Compromised.

As You Proclaim the Truth, remember that It is Not Personal — It is Just the TRUTH. People are not necessarily upset at you; It is the *God In You* that they will not admit that they are upset with. The principles of Grace and Mercy Can Cover wrongdoing without Compromising TRUTH. However, remember that Grace and Mercy Do Not Change the TRUTH.

~ Grace and Mercy **DO NOT CHANGE** the TRUTH.

~ Grace and Mercy "Compliment" the TRUTH.

~ Grace and Mercy Shines a Glowing Spotlight on the TRUTH.

The Prophetic Anointing in You is Like a Magnet, and it attracts the Good and the Bad.

<u>The Prophetic Anointing in You Attracts:</u>
- Intrigue
- Respect
- Competition
- Love
- Hate
- Enmity
  (The state or feeling of being actively opposed or hostile to someone or something.)
- Criticism
- Ridicule
- Mocking

Be encouraged – Because when You Draw Backlash, it is an indicator, a sign that the God of TRUTH is Dethroning every idol, every lie, and The Spirit of TRUTH is ascending to position Himself on the Throne.

CHAPTER SEVEN

Walk in Dominion

The Promise Line, The Plumbline and Your Kingdom Attitude of Dominion
Zechariah 4:9-10

The Promise line and the plumb line work together to form the foundation of your kingdom attitude of Dominion. In order to understand this principle, it would be helpful to examine each concept separately. Let us take a closer look at the concept of the *"Promise Line."* The Promise line is the Father's heart spoken and written in covenant with you. The word covenant is important because God's covenant is better than a contract. A covenant is something he will never break, no matter what the circumstances.

Let us look closer at the spoken covenant Promise line. Imagine the Father whispering quietly in your ears. He does so every time you pray and are in conversation with him. The Lord whispers in your ear every day, throughout the day, revealing himself and his secrets to you. Sometimes we miss these intimate encounters because we are distracted or are not yet intimately familiar with the sound or pattern of his voice. Yet his voice there faithfully every day to help us along our way. His spoken covenant serves as simple everyday reassurances. His spoken covenant to us serves as simple everyday guideposts.

Just as God's spoken covenant represents his promise line, so does His written word. His written promises "Leap' from the pages of inspiration. His written word provides encouragement and renewal. **His written Word is the Manna we eat every day.** The written promise line is there for exploration. It is there for deep exploration to reveal Truth and the pathway to life and success. The written Word is a powerful tool to help you live a life of Dominion.

Are You Familiar with the written Promises? Have you read the Contract...The Covenant? Has God's Will been read to you? Do You Know Your Rights? Do You Know what your Inheritance is? In order to promote your understanding of the covenant, let us revisit a few Promise line scriptures.

John 3:16 ~ *This scripture serves as the fundamental foundational promise of the Father to all those who will accept the gift of Salvation through his son Jesus Christ. The promises associated with becoming a member of the heavenly family are many. Everlasting life is just the first of many.*

Psalms 91 ~ *represents an entirely different portion of the written promise. It is that of divine protection.*

Philippians 4:7 ~ *Highlights the promise of Divine Peace.*

John 14:27 ~ *Highlights the same Concept of Divine Peace*

Deuteronomy 28:13 *Highlights the promise of Dominion. The promise of being the Head, not the tail.*

Even a surface-level understanding of the Promises of God can make one jump with excitement. David said it best in Psalm 139:6 *"Such knowledge for me is too wonderful for me… Too Lofty for to Attain".*

Now that we have developed a foundation for the Promise line, let us transition to focus upon understanding the concept of the ***"Plumb line."*** The Plumb line is literally a vertical reference line to ensure that a structure is centered. It is used during construction to ensure that the work is appropriately aligned…that the structure is straight. The Prophet Zechariah uses the concept of the Plumb line to speak spiritual truth.

"Who despises the Day of small "Things"? Men will rejoice when they see "The Plumb line" in the hand of Zerubbabel." Zechariah 4: 9-10

In your life, what is it that is small in the eyes of man that causes you to "Think" small, to think that what you are doing is insignificant? The principle of the Plumbline is the principle of beginnings. It is an indicator that things are in construction mode. During construction, only the architect can fully envision the finished state of the structure. During the construction process, others can only see unfinished construction. Outsiders do not have the blueprints, so they cannot envision the finished state, nor can they appreciate the value of the building process. To outsiders, things may appear messy and unorganized. However, you must understand that your heavenly Father is the holder of the Plumb line, and that HE is constructing something beautiful.

Let us take a closer look at the *"Plumb line principle"* in action. As we review this principle in action in the lives of two of our favorite old testament heroes, we will feel encouraged to embrace the "Plumb Line" with increased levels of expectation. The improbable journeys of Joseph and King David leave us inspired. Let us explore each.

Joseph
Entered Egypt as a slave and was wrongly accused throughout his time in Potiphar's house. Early on, his ability to interpret dreams appeared of no value. However, this seemingly insignificant ability led him from the prison to the palace.

King David
His seemingly routine journey to deliver lunch to his older brothers, became a Divine appointment for him to Deliver the Israelites from the hand of the Philistines and an arrogant, condescending Giant.

Joseph and Mary
Gave birth in a "Barn" to a child whose legacy would unite the rift between God and Man that had existed since the Garden of Eden.

12 Disciples
Twelve Unlearned and ordinary men lead the Greatest Revolution the World has ever seen.

The Promise Line and the Plumb line are components of the formula for a winning attitude, an attitude of Dominion.
Embrace Your Dominion!

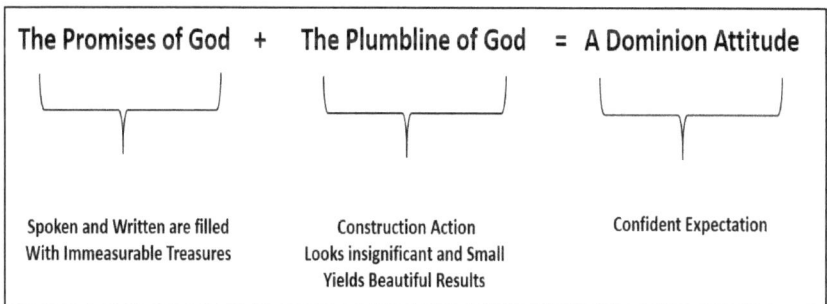

The Promises of God +	The Plumbline of God =	A Dominion Attitude
Spoken and Written are filled With Immeasurable Treasures	Construction Action Looks insignificant and Small Yields Beautiful Results	Confident Expectation

And God blessed them, and God said unto them, Be fruitful, and multiply, and replenish the earth, and subdue it: and have dominion over the fish of the sea, and over the fowl of the air, and over every living thing that moveth upon the earth. Genesis 1:28 (KJV)

Can These Dry Bones Live?
Ezekiel 37:1-14

In the passage above, The Lord asked the Prophet Ezekiel about a situation that literally had no Life, no Hope. In other words, the bones the Prophet saw were dead and had been dead for a long time. The bones were evidence that, at one time, Life existed within them. What is interesting about the question posed to Ezekiel is that it "challenged" his perspective. Was there Hope of Life for the Dead Bones?

EVERYDAY GOD CHALLENGES OUR PERSPECTIVE
Obviously, the bones were dry and dead. Common sense asserts that there was no hope of life ever returning to the dead situation the Prophet saw. However, God was not really asking the Prophet to see the situation and answer the question through mere human common sense. The Lord God "provoked" the Prophet to "S.E.E." through the eyes of Faith. God wanted Ezekiel to Believe not in what he saw with his human eyes or believe in his own human capacity to revive the dead situation but to "Believe" that his God possessed more power than the hopelessness of a dead situation.

We all encounter hopeless and dead situations every day. The question God has for us is the same question He had for Ezekiel… "Can These Dry Bones Live?" How we answer that question reveals both our perspective and our true level of Faith in an Almighty God. As with Ezekiel, Our Father God continuously challenges our perspective and provokes our Faith.

How are you looking at the situations that appear Hopeless in Your Life?

What do you have in your hands to bring life to those things that appear hopeless? Have others come to YOU to help with things that are hopeless in their lives? What things in society that appear hopeless provoke you? Do you have God's perspective or your own regarding these things?

GOD COMMANDED EZEKIEL TO SPEAK…

Not only did God challenge Ezekiel's perspective and provoke his Faith, but God also commanded Ezekiel to "Speak." In other words, "God propelled Ezekiel into action." It is important to understand that it is great to have God's perspective, and it is great to have Faith, but without action, these things fall flat. God commanded Ezekiel to speak, and when Ezekiel spoke, things began to move. That is action. **Is there Action behind Your Faith?** Is there Action behind the things that you believe? In the passage, we see something peculiar. When Ezekiel begins to Speak, God begins to Move things …set things in motion.

You see, as it was with Ezekiel, Our Faith in Action is the Catalyst for God to Move.
God asks again, "Can These Dry Bones Live?"
The answer is a resounding YES!!!

Then he said to me, "Prophesy to these bones and say to them, 'Dry bones, hear the word of the Lord! This is what the Sovereign Lord says to these bones: I will make breath enter you, and you will come to life.
Ezekiel 37:4-5 (NIV)

Rally the Troops and Release the Mission Mindset
Joshua1:3,6,8 ~ Joshua 3:10 ~ Joshua 4:13

Through this devotional, you both see and hear the Call. You are maturing and ready to move. You have a thorough understanding of the value of brokenness. You are willing to Face Yourself. Your heart is in the right posture. You are willing to take the Hit. Those were six essential stages needed to journey through this process to prompt you to use, *What is in Your Hands.*

The seventh and final step of this Journey is to Rally and Release The Mission Mindset. "Get ready, get moving; I am giving you the Land." This is essentially what God told Joshua. This same message is relevant and is to YOU today:
"Get ready, get moving; I am giving you the Land."

God says, "Tell my people that they are well equipped for the assignment in the territory I have given them. Reestablish the boundary lines, lay claim to the promises of the previous generation. Where there is despair, declare Hope. Reveal to my people the Beauty of this Promised Land, My land. It is a Good land, a fertile land, to live and to Grow. Remove the squatters (Spiritual and otherwise). RE-ESTABLISH, REACTIVATE, POLISH, RENEW EXTEND. These are MY PEOPLE, and I have NOT Forgotten Them. **BUILD, MULTIPLE, LAY HOLD and COMPLETE THE VISION."**

In the passage above in verse eight, God further highlights to Joshua, "Do not worry, You will be Prosperous and Successful... Be STRONG and COURAGEOUS and do not forget my protocols my law". This same message is to us, **"Do not worry, everything will be O.K. but Be Strong."**

Along the journey, God knew that Joshua would face some very terrible, arduous situations in order to obtain the Promise of the "Promise Land." The situation is the same with us. **God's Promise to You has <u>NOT </u>Changed**. Dig Deep, Standfast, BE STRONG and pursue the Promise for Your Life, the life of your family, the life of your Community. God told Joshua, "Do not be Scared... Do not Be Intimidated... Do not Be Discouraged. God was "with" Joshua. The word "with" is important for it denotes God's presence, his Favor, and his Power. It denoted the Full entity of Everything that God is was "with" Joshua. *GOD is With Us Also*.

Project into the Future ~ Every Promise is fulfilled

One of the most astonishing statements in the Book of Joshua is highlighted in chapter 23, verse

14.   Joshua is older and has conquered and possessed the "Promised Land." In the passage, he has essentially come to the end of his life and spends this last public moment to *remind* the People of Israel that "**God Kept His Promises.**" Think about that for a moment... God Kept His Promises; throughout all the challenge and turmoil, God Kept His Promises. If God Kept His Promises to Joshua, He will Keep His Promises to You...

Go Conquer the Land and Inherit the Promise!!!

...You know with all your heart and soul that not one of all the good promises the Lord your God gave you has failed. Every promise has been fulfilled; not one has failed. Joshua 23:14

CHAPTER EIGHT

New Season

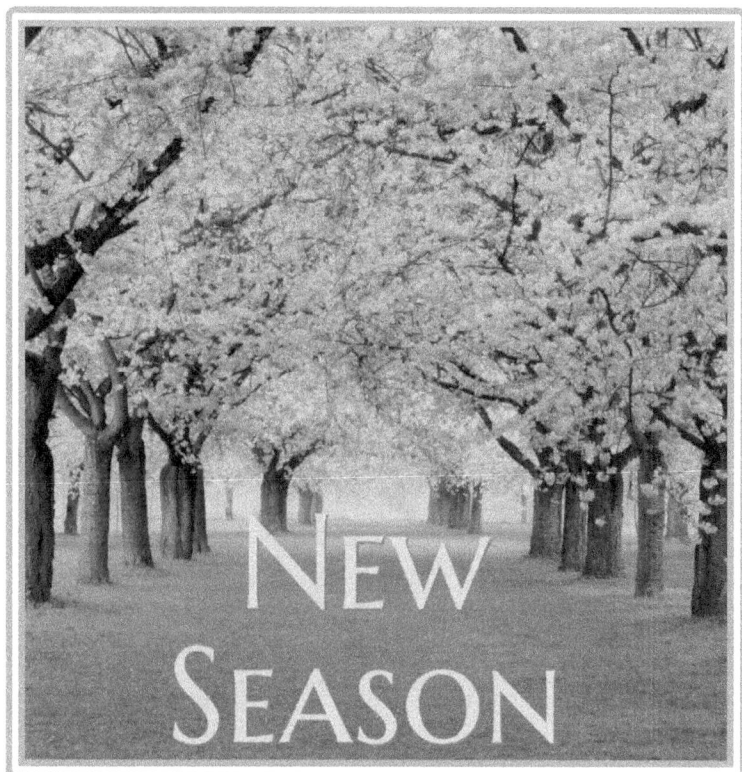

Get Ready; Your Father is About to Validate You Openly

Matthew 17:1–8 ~ Mark 9:2–8

The path higher is steep, but Glory is at the top if you are willing to climb. Just as Jesus chose Peter, James, and John to climb the mountain, in the same manner, God chose *YOU* to Climb Higher. At the top, there awaited Transfiguration. As God's servant, Jesus was transfigured so that he could "Complete" the work his Father assigned him here on Earth.

"Get Ready; Your Father is About to Validate You Openly"

You chose to See, Hear and Adhere to the Shofar Call. You have journeyed through the chapters of this book and received both "Revelation and Activation." Do not look now, but You are Glowing**.**

Your Face is Shining…Your Clothes are Glowing

In the passage above, as Jesus was communing with the Father, he began to Shine! He shined so bright that it left Peter, James, and John speechless. Yes, You are Shining in Revelation and Activation!

Shine Bright!!!

Shining Bright seems to be a common occurrence among those who have spent intimate time with the Father. Recall in Exodus chapter 34, when Moses came down the mountain with the two tablets of the covenant law; he was radiant; he was shining so brightly that the people requested him to veil his face.

"Get Ready; Your Father is About to Speak on Your Behalf"

In the passage, as Jesus shined radiantly while Peter, James, and John looked upon him in total astonishment, God the Father began to speak on his behalf. It was a "Validation" from the highest Authority.

While he was still speaking, a bright cloud covered them, and a voice from the cloud said, "This is my Son, whom I love; with him, I am well pleased. Listen to him!" Matthew 17:5

You are not only God's Servant, but you are His Daughter, His Son… His Beloved. As you use What is in Your Hand to Build His Kingdom, HE IS WELL PLEASED WITH YOU. In the same manner that he validated Jesus on the mountain amid Peter, James, and John, He Validates YOU.

So…*"Get Ready, Your Father is About to Validate You Openly"*

_____

_____

_____

_____

_____

_____

_____

_____

_____

_____

_____

_____

_____

_____

_____

_____

The Seemingly Small Insignificant Thing
Zechariah 4:10~ Matthew 13:31–32 ~ John 6:9 ~
I Corinthians 1:26-29

You have already considered the principle of "The Small Thing"; however, let us revisit this principle again as you prepare to depart and complete your time on the mountain top inside the cave with Your Heavenly Father. Revelation has *already* been *activated* within you, so we will allow the Holy Spirit to speak directly to you regarding the scriptures above. Here is what they proclaim.

"Who dares despise the day of small things…
Zechariah 4:10

Matthew 13:31–32   He told them another parable: "The kingdom of heaven is like a mustard seed, which a man took and planted in his field. 32 Though it is the smallest of all seeds, yet when it grows, it is the largest of garden plants and becomes a tree, so that the birds come and perch in its branches."

"Here is a boy with five small barley loaves and two small fish, but how far will they go among so many?" John 6:9

I Corinthians 1:26-29   Brothers and sisters think of

what you were when you were called. Not many of you were wise by human standards; not many were influential; not many were of noble birth. 27 But God chose the foolish things of the world to shame the wise; God chose the weak things of the world to shame the strong. 28 God chose the lowly things of this world and the despised things—and the things that are not—to nullify the things that are, 29 so that no one may boast before him.

This is What Your Father Says to YOU Today

It is the seemingly small insignificant, and mostly ignored things that I work miracles through. Readily accept whom I have called you to be. I HAVE ALREADY APPROVED YOU! You are my beloved child, whom I Love Deeply. The simplest things you yearn for I will give to you. It is my pleasure to give what you ask.

REST IN MY PROVIDENCE; I WILL NOT FAIL YOU... REST IN MY LOVE, GRACE, AND ACCEPTANCE.

New Season
II Corinthians 5:17~ Isaiah 43:18-19

THE OLD HAS PASSED AWAY; THE NEW HAS COME!
Today You are FREE to be Whom Your Father has "Called" You to Be.

Forget the former things; do not dwell on the past. See, I am doing a new thing! Now it springs up; do you not perceive it? I am making a way in the wilderness and streams in the wasteland.   Isaiah 43:18-19

Your Eyes are Open. Your Ears are Open. Your Heart is Pure. Your Spirit is Strong.   Your Face is Shining. Your Clothes are Radiant.   Now You are Ready! Walk in FREEDOM!!!

Freedom Declaration
Today I am FREE!!!
I am Free in my mind and heart to live with no pre-ordained constraints.
You have told me, Father, to walk in the liberty wherewith you have made me free and not to be entangled again with the yoke of bondage.
Father, you have said that you knew me before I was born, even before I was in my mother's womb. Before my parents gave me a name, Lord, You named me. Before I took on my race and gender, you knew me and made me Free, and gave me Purpose.

Before my intellect could be measured and before the possibilities of what I could be in life could be framed by limitation, you had already granted me my FREEDOM and gave me Purpose!!! Before Anyone could indoctrinate my mind, heart, and soul with the Doctrine of Bondage, and the Principal of Limitation, You had already created in me a Seed of inheritance this is Incorruptible. TODAY, Father, I am FREE! I rise. I shake off Limitation and Constraint. I allow scales to fall from my eyes so that I can SEE as You SEE.

TODAY, I walk into the Destiny that You had Already Ordained for Me before the World and World Systems could begin to lay snares of doubt and limitation.

THANK YOU, FATHER, FOR WHO YOU ARE AND FOR THE POWER OF YOUR "PURPOSE AND FREEDOM"! TODAY, I use What is in My Hands !!!

BOOK REVIEWS

In reading Dr. Temaki Carr's devotional *the following comes to mind:*

And unto one He gave five talents, to another two, and to another one; to every man according to his several ability; and straightway took His journey Matthew 25:15

The time has come when we must become busy for our Lord. We each have something that has been given to us as Blessings for someone.   Often while meditating on my upbringing and subsequent life, I say to our Father God, "Father, I thank You for placing me in the Shines family. I thank You for every teacher that You destined to teach me, for every neighbor who was kind, and for every Church Family who prayed, chastised, encouraged me.
I thank You Father for every student who challenged me and for every thankful student who still corresponds.
These "helps" were in their hands ranging from sums of money to pouting faces.

Remember: What you have in your hands does not belong to you.

-E. Jeanne Polk, LPC, NCC-

Thanks for reading! Please add a short review on Amazon.com and let me know what you thought!

BOOK REVIEWS

Dr. Temaki Carr's devotional, "What Do You Have in Your Hands," delivers a blessing converting hard earned experience into nuggets of godly wisdom. Her focused Biblical teachings engage us with shareable gems of actionable and spiritual intelligence. The aim is to help others see truth, reflect on one's own condition, and move toward one's true calling and godly purpose.

Dr. Carr strives to transform our comfort in the status quo and organized apathy into effective progress for this side of Heaven. She is not interested in the ordinary, but instead for us each to pursue the extraordinary and anointed calling of being in step with the Creator. As He gifted each of us uniquely, we must seek, exalt, and expect the Lord to be with us, for us, and ahead of us. We must ignore the world's promises and be willing to be uncomfortable in walking into our Kingdom purpose.

-Laura Hart, Community Organizer, Realtor-

Thanks for reading! Please add a short review on Amazon.com

and let me know what you thought!

ABOUT THE AUTHOR

Temaki Carr, Founder & CEO of "Loving The Nations" Missions Ministry, is a Strategist, Community Organizer, Chief Executive, Faith Builder, Truth Teller, Humanitarian, Philanthropist, Veteran, Leader, and Servant. These are just a few of the attributes which describe, Temaki Carr. Her life experiences has journeyed through poverty stricken wooden shacks of Mississippi to palatial palaces of foreign dictators in war-torn countries. From the "Battlefield" to the "Mission Field" she has journeyed through remote villages and overpopulated city squares in western Africa to isolated communities in the Himalayan mountains of Nepal to the narrow streets of old world Europe. She is a Trailblazer with a unique passion and ability to cross cultural divides to uplift and inspire.

Born the eldest of four children to widower Doris Funchess of Prentiss, Mississippi, Temaki Carr became the first of her maternal family to accept Christ, astonishingly doing so at the tender age of 12 years old. Temaki continued the trend of firsts, trailblazing as the first within her family to attend and graduate college. Upon completion of undergraduate studies from Southern University in Baton Rouge, Louisiana, Temaki was commissioned a Second Lieutenant in the United States Army.

During her 20-year active duty tenure, Lieutenant Colonel (Ret) Temaki Carr served in leadership positions throughout the Continental United States and abroad leading soldiers in both peace and war. Throughout the entirety of her active-duty tenure, she served together with her husband of 28 years, Colonel Robert Carr, facing the tumultuous challenges associated with the lifestyle of a dual military family. Throughout this time, she endeavored to maintain a sense of service excellence to her God, her Family, and her Country.

Temaki Carr holds a Bachelor of Arts in Broadcast Communications, a Master of Divinity in Inter-Cultural Relations and a Doctor of Ministry in Community Organizing. The Reverend Dr. Temaki Carr serves as a licensed and ordained clergyman, with over 30 years of ministerial service. The Reverend Dr. Carr is also Apostle Carr. Apostle Dr. Carr is a proud proponent of the Fivefold Ministry, believing that the operation of Fivefold gifts are critical to the Kingdom of God in this hour.

Apostle Dr. Carr is the founder and Chief Executive Officer of *Loving the Nations*, a 501c3 charitable organization specializing in global missions, evangelism, education, humanitarian aid and community organizing. With partner ministries in Nepal, Pakistan, Africa, Europe and the United States, *Loving the Nations* endeavors not only to equip and mobilize the Global Church to fulfill the Great Commission but to do so as a unified force serving the nations in love.

Amid the growing racial divide in America, and believing change begins with the Church, Apostle Dr. Carr has co-founded "One Church Rappahannock Region" and "Undivided Fredericksburg" in order to promote racial reconciliation within the household of Faith.

For the past 28 years Dr. Temaki Carr has been happily married to Colonel Robert Carr. They have three lovely daughters, Dominique, a 26-year-old graduate of Virginia

Commonwealth University, Danielle, a 23-year-old graduate of Manhatanville College in White plains New York, and Gabrielle, a 21-year-old Junior at the University of Virginia.

Connect with Dr. Temaki Carr on:

Facebook: @Loving The Nations

Website: Www. LovingTheNations.org

Email: LovingTheNationsBooks@gmail.com